Peter Tchaikovsky

AND THE NUTCRACKER BALLET

By

Opal Wheeler

Illustrated by Christine Price

Zeezok PUBLISHING

Peter Tchaikovsky and the Nutcracker Ballet
Written by Opal Wheeler

Originally published by E.P. Dutton & Company, New York, 1959.
Copyright © 1959, by Opal Wheeler.

ISBN 978-1-61006-012-7
Copyright © 2011 by Zeezok Publishing, LLC
Published August, 2017
Printed in the United States of America

Zeezok Publishing, LLC
PO Box 1960 • Elyria, OH 44036
info@Zeezok.com • 1-800-749-1681

www.Zeezok.com

Peter Tchaikovsky
AND THE NUTCRACKER BALLET

CHAPTER ONE

The troika bells pierced the January darkness with their silvery clingety-clang, clingety-clang. Around the corner and up the hill they rang more slowly as the horses pulled the long sleigh through the snowy streets.

"Petia! The Moscow coach is here! Hurry!"

The twins raced to the door to pile the bags and bundles of their beloved older brother into the arms of the waiting servant.

"Moscow! On to Moscow!" they shouted, pulling on long greatcoats as they ran into the icy courtyard.

"Goodbye! Goodbye!" Aunts, uncles, and cousins filled Peter's hands with tidbits for the journey as he stood in the doorway, ready to leave.

"Heaven knows we shall miss you, my son." Ilya brushed the tears from his eyes. "God keep you safe and happy and bring you success in your new work."

"Petia! Petia!" The calls were far down the street, and Peter's long legs followed after the twins. Now and then he turned and waved to the dear ones behind, calling back his goodbyes as he ran.

The boys were holding the coach, and the driver was grumbling into his beard as Peter climbed aboard.

"Always a passenger late while we freeze to death."

The door slammed behind him, and panting from his run, Peter fell into a seat beside a dark plump woman. Sudden shrill barking filled the coach, and the next moment, strong arms flung him into the aisle.

"Oh, oh, my Tou-Tou! You have sat on my poor dear little Tou-Tou! Yes, almost you have finished her. Monster!"

The angry woman lifted the toy animal to her cheek,

stroking it and murmuring endearing words into the tiny ears.

Peter looked down at her helplessly.

"1 am sorry, so sorry, Madame," he stammered. "There seemed to be only a folded blanket on the seat. If only I could help–"

At the torrent of bitter words from her lips, he fled to the only place left. The handsome young man next to him was shaking with silent laughter.

"This is the third experience for small Tou-Tou," he explained. "Must be a sturdy little beastie." Quietly he turned to watch the small creature. "Have no fear. It is as frisky as a lamb on a bright spring morning."

He held out a box of beautifully decorated cakes to Peter.

"Good food eases the mind, my friend. Eat plentifully."

The dapper stranger placed the tin between them, and the two munched the excellent cakes in silence as the sleigh coach made its slow way over the icy roads.

"Are you traveling far?"

"To Moscow, where I visited long ago as a boy."

The stranger nodded. "Wish I could be as lucky. I start work as a lawyer in a small town nearby, in the office of a crochety old uncle."

Peter turned to him sharply,

"A lawyer did you say? I, too, studied for long years to become one, just to please my good father. But I was not much use, especially on the day I was asked to take a very important document to an official for the gold seal of state. In the warm, lazy sunshine, the loveliest melodies kept running through my mind, and as I strolled along, the paper tapped against my lips. By the time I reached the building, I found to my horror that I had eaten almost the entire document!"

Hearty laughter rang through the coach, and the stranger turned merry eyes on his companion.

"You must have been hungry, indeed, my friend."

"Yes, hungry for music." Peter's face lighted suddenly.

"Soon afterward, my father consented to my leaving the offices and studying music with the great master, Anton Rubinstein. And now, after a year of work, the adventure of a whole lifetime is before me. Think of it," he cried, "I go to the new school of his brother, to teach pupils how to set down their melodies."

"Then you must write music yourself."

"Oh, yes. Night and day melodies burn in my mind and give me no peace until I have scribbled them on paper." Peter grinned happily. "Would you believe it? Not long ago, the master Johann Strauss conducted my 'Peasant Dances.'"

The young lawyer sat up quickly, grasping the arm of his companion.

"In the park in St. Petersburg, this past summer? But my dear fellow, I was there, myself, shouting with the audience under the skies for more of the gay music! Then you must be Peter Tchaikovsky!"

Solemnly he held out his hand and shook Peter's warmly.

"My compliments, sir. No wonder you are making music your life's work."

The carriage came to a halt with a sharp lurch.

"My station so soon!" Quickly the young lawyer gathered his belongings together and left the coach, calling after him, "Farewell, and good luck to the new life of music."

The time passed slowly now, and the bitter wind howled like a demon in distress, creeping into every nook and corner of the worn, creaking sleigh.

There was need of comfort, indeed, as through the hours the coach lurched in and out of the deep ruts in the roadway. Peter closed his eyes, trying to see in his mind the faces of those he had left at home. Modka and Tolka. Their bright smiles made the tears creep from under his eyelids. Peter shook them away and sighed. If only he could have seen them again before the coach started.

The miles of roadway stretched on and on. Would they never end?

"First station change! Everyone out!"

Numb with the cold, Peter stumbled to the door and was about to board the new coach when strong young arms seized him from behind.

"Petia!"

Peter gasped. Surely he must be dreaming. There, before him, shivering with the cold, were the twins!

"How–where—why–" he began lamely, shaking his head in dismay.

The boys shrieked with delight at their plot.

"We rode in the back, with the baggage! It was freezing!" they cried, rubbing their red noses with icy fingers. Suddenly quiet, they looked up hopefully. "Please, Petia, you will take us with you to Moscow?" they begged.

At the stern frown on their brother's brow, they turned on their heels and made a dash for the coach. But Peter was too quick for them. His long legs overtook them, and seizing them by the coat collars, he shook them, scolding them roundly.

"Rascals! Vagabonds! You would play tricks on me when you should be back in school? And poor old father–what will he think when he finds you gone? Answer me, young blackguards!"

The look of sadness was too much for Peter, and the next moment his arms were around the young shoulders in a warm hug.

"Ah, my children, nothing would gladden my heart more than to take you with me," he declared. Suddenly he raised his head at the warning whistle. "Quickly!" he ordered. "Back to St. Petersburg with you both!"

Pushing them into the returning coach, he waved them off, calling laughingly, "Rascals! Begone!"

Climbing into his own sleigh, he started on the last leg of his journey, happier than he had been for long hours. With a coin he scratched a little hole through the thick frost on the windowpane and watched the countryside fly by.

Huts and farmhouses struggled to free themselves from the snowbanks that stretched on and on over the vast steppes that seemed never to end. One by one the windows began to glow like tiny candles in the early winter dusk.

Moscow at last! Stretching his cold, aching legs, Peter found himself in the great city. Hundreds of church bells over his head sang their blessings to the night, just as they had done when he had come as a boy.

Newly fallen snow silenced his footfalls as he trod the streets, his belongings slung over his shoulders. Watchdogs in darkened courtyards sprang at him now and then with throaty growls, to be silenced with a few quiet words.

"So, old Druids, you cannot frighten me with all your huffing and puffing. I am your good friend, remember?"

All around, merry troika bells on harnesses sang their little songs as horses trotted briskly along with snugly-blanketed passengers. Peter breathed deeply the clear frosty air. How good it was to be in the bustling city again with its sights and sounds.

Peering carefully at doormarkers, he at last found the Rubinstein home on a narrow side street. At his knock, the door opened speedily, and there stood a handsome man, a smile of welcome lighting his face.

"Ah, you must be young Tchaikovsky! And frozen to the bone, I declare. Come in, my good fellow, come in! My brother, Anton, has told me many fine things about you."

Into the crowded hallway Nicholas Rubinstein led his new teacher, talking all the while.

"The payment for your services will be very little, as you know, with the music school just beginning. So of course you will not mind living here with us, in our home," he explained. "Ah, here we are, in your cozy little quarters. I hope you will be very happy."

Happy! Peter looked in dismay at the close, cramped narrow room lighted by a tiny window high in the wall. Surely he would not be here for long.

There was little time for worry, with lessons beginning at once in the same house. Peter was given the proud title of Professor of Theory and Composition, and he worked hard all day long in helping young students to write their melodies. Patient and kind he was, and Nicholas was pleased, indeed, and soon found him to be the best teacher in his new school.

"The work is good, Tchaikovsky!" he exclaimed one morning, after watching his new professor. "A stone could not help learning from you." He smiled brightly. "But all work is not good. You shall go with me this very evening to a musical party. Elegant it will be, and you will hear many fine artists play for the entertainment. "

One look at his young professor told him that all was not well.

"But sir, I–I could not be a part of an elegant gathering in this attire." Peter flushed more deeply, his eyes on his shabby, worn clothing.

Nicholas quickly put a hand on the thin shoulder of his hungry young teacher.

"Ah, my friend, we shall soon remedy such a small lack. Follow me, sir!"

Gaily he led the way to a little guest room and opened a closet door.

"See what good fortune awaits you! The raiment of my friend, the famous Polish violinist, Henri Wieniavsky. He has left them here for over a year. So now they are yours, Tchaikovsky. It is the law of the land."

Laughing merrily, he held the evening coat for Peter. But the shoulders were much too large, and the trousers fell in great wrinkles around his ankles.

"Straighten up, son! 'Twill hold everything in place"

A shirt and hat from Rubinstein's own wardrobe made the costume complete. But all through the evening Peter was miserable, indeed, keeping his shoulders so erect that they ached sorely.

Many kindnesses there were at the hand of the famous pianist, Rubinstein, who grew ever more fond of his young professor as the months flew swiftly by. And hard Peter worked to repay his friend, struggling from morning until night with groups of young pupils. Only after darkness had fallen was he permitted to seek his little room, to put down his own melodies that turned round and round in his mind.

In the midst of the racing notes one night, he stopped in dismay. How he had neglected his younger brothers! He must write to them at once, telling them of his new life. Hastily the words fell onto the paper.

Dear Modka and Tolka,

I have a little room next to Rubinstein's bedroom, and am quite afraid of disturbing him with the scratching of my pen. I sit at home, scarcely ever going out. But you should see Rubinstein! He is always rushing here and there. He thinks I am a very hard worker. I cannot help being lonely at times, but my thirst for work consoles me. Yesterday I was upset at the thought of the first night after the holidays, with Modka's head under the bedclothes to hide his tears. How I longed to comfort him, poor child! Modka, I bid you to study, study, and study some more. And do be careful to choose good fellows to be your friends. Sweet Tolka, overcome your laziness and send me a letter. A kiss for you both.

Poor Peter. Even in his own room, never could he work in peace. Scales and exercises and the tooting of instruments sounded just outside, and he held his head in his hands at the fearful noise. Every little while, calls and thumpings at his door made him jump from his chair.

"Tchaikovsky! Come and hear the new Mozart Sonata that I will play at my next concert. My pupil is ready. You must listen to his Beethoven. The musical tea is at five. Be sure that you do not forget."

One morning, waking very early, Peter lay in his bed, thinking happily of the free hours that had come by surprise. Suddenly an idea came to him. Bounding from his narrow cot, he dressed quickly and rolled some paper into a bundle. Now if only he could slip away from the house without being discovered, all would be well.

Holding his shoes in his hand, he crept down the long stairs and opened the creaking door slowly. Out in the blinding snowstorm, he laughed softly. He was free, free, free! Quickly he swung down the street in the early dawn, tiny hard snow pellets biting into his face as he broke into a happy song.

On and around the corner he went and soon found himself at the door of an inn. The old porter, sweeping under the empty tables, looked up at him sleepily.

"Bit early fer eatin', young feller. Cook's off fer a bit o' snoozin'. Wait if ye like."

Peter smiled his thanks and swiftly unrolled his paper on a table in the corner.

"A place to work is all I need for the moment, my good man."

The old servant rubbed a worn shoe against the other.

"Plenty o' empty tables fer company." He looked closely at Peter for a moment and reached into his back pocket. "Ye look a mite hungry, son. Here, have a good bite, jest for luck."

Peter eyed the grimy black sausage in the hardened palm and hastily shook his head.

"You are very kind. But I am not at all hungry."

Turning swiftly to the table, he began to work with his pen in the dim candlelight. To the quiet swish, swish of the broom, the notes of his first symphony fell thickly onto the paper. On and on he scratched away, his eyes bright, his breath coming short and fast. How the melodies sang in his mind!

Noon customers began to saunter in for a good hot meal. Rolling up his scattered sheets, Peter hurried home for a bit of cold food before beginning afternoon classes.

His new teacher friend, Kashkin, looked at him sharply as they took their places at the noisy table.

"So the runaway has returned," said he, nodding his bushy head. "All morning long I have searched for you to play Wagner music with me."

"Sh! Do not give away my secret, Kashkin! Come with me a half hour before work begins, and you will know what I have been doing."

The small meal was speedily eaten, and the two stole away to a back room where a piano stood ready. His hands trembling with excitement, Peter spread the new music on the rack.

"See, Kashkin! How much of my first symphony was done in just one morning!"

Playing and singing parts here and there, the young composer ran through the music, stopping to explain now and then.

Peter shouted his joy, his hands crashing on the keys in a broad chord that echoed through the little room. Leaping to his feet, he grasped the astonished Kashkin by the shoulders.

"Oh, my friend, there is so much melody here, and here, that it gives me pain," he cried, striking his head and chest.

Pains there were, indeed, that grew steadily worse. To Rubinstein went the faithful Kashkin, telling the master his fears.

"Poor, dear Peter," sighed the noted pianist, stroking his chin. "There is nothing in all the world that I would not do to help him. Such musical promise I have never seen in one so young." He paused a moment. "Kashkin, I have it!" he declared suddenly. "When we see the trouble coming again, we will give our friend a shock, and the pains will be forgotten in a hurry."

The two plotted together in low tones, working out their little scheme to cure their beloved comrade.

That evening, just after the early dinner was finished, Peter suddenly placed his hand on his stomach, his eyes dark with pain. One look at the victim and the plotters slipped quietly from the room.

Stealing behind the door, they slammed it shut with a terrible clap, and leaping into the air, screamed and yelled into the sufferer's ears with all their might.

Peter looked up at them in amazement.

"Has the devil got you, then?" he asked, still holding his poor stomach.

The weeks wore on, and when the pain did not leave, the doctor was called.

"So," he murmured, watching his new patient carefully. "I believe we have the answer. Too much work, young man. You must give up your night composing."

Peter shook his head in despair. "Give up my writing! That would be to tell me to stop breathing!"

It was well that the summer was near at hand. The school would soon close, and the last days seemed never to end. The minutes were like hours, and his students, who loved their teacher dearly, hung on every word.

"Above all, do not forget your music while you are away, young gentlemen." Peter stood before them, tall and handsome in threadbare clothing, his serious blue eyes searching their faces. "I beg you to waste no precious minutes. When the autumn arrives, you shall bring back to me a fine composition of your own making. Let there be no idleness!"

They were gone, and behind him, Rubinstein and the other young teachers were shouting laughingly in his ears.

"Let there be nothing BUT idleness for you, Peter!"

Before he could answer, they seized him by the arms and led him to the door, chanting, "No compositions, no compositions!" Into the waiting carriage they pushed him, where he discovered his bags, all carefully packed, on the seat beside him.

The door was shut by his laughing comrades, and he was on his way. Peter waved at them feebly and sank back, breathless.

"Why, I believe they like me very much!" he found himself speaking aloud.

An old man near him smiled and pulled a fringed shawl closer around his shoulders in the chilly dusk.

"Like you, young man? Why, I'd give a whole litter of white rabbits if my own kin cared half as much!"

To be at home again! Home, home, home! The word sang in his mind and heart as he jogged along.

And never was a summer more glorious for Peter. At the end of the long months, he was rested, indeed. But only because his first symphony, his dearest child, was finished. Not only finished, but on its way to his old master, Anton Rubinstein.

It would be hard to wait for an answer. How proud he would be of his pupil! Peter smiled happily at the thought as he walked about, teaching his Moscow students again. All the cares of the world seemed to have vanished. Soon, now, he would be earning more, especially when the new symphony was printed. Then he could move to a house of his own, where there would be no noise, and he could compose in peace to his heart's content.

This plaintive little song of Peter's will sing itself in your mind, long after you have heard it.

A SONG OF SADNESS

Allegro non troppo

"Mail! Mail for Peter Tchaikovsky!" Peter heard a heavy package drop at his door. Opening it swiftly, his eyes lighted. It had come! The great master had sent back the symphony!

With trembling hands, Peter tore off the covering. But one look at the words of his old teacher and his heart sank within him.

For long minutes he sat alone, his head buried in his arms, all hope gone. But suddenly he raised his eyes, a fierce resolve rising within him. Never again would he ask anyone for help with his compositions! He would write as he felt, in his own way.

As the days wore on, he found himself going over parts of the new work. Perhaps it could be better. Ah yes, this little place needed strengthening. And what were the flutes doing there? Much better to have the violins playing the section.

Now it was truly finished. Off it went to the printer, and when the news arrived that it would be played by the great Moscow symphony orchestra, Peter's joy knew no bounds. But as quickly, a sudden fear clutched at his heart.

"Nobody knows the poor struggling composer!" he cried, eating not a mouthful of the food before him. "So of course no one will come to hear the symphony! There is no use going to the auditorium,"

Nicholas Rubinstein laughed at his badly upset professor.

"Then the teachers of the Rubinstein Conservatory of Music will be the audience. Forward, friends! To the concert hall!"

They were going to play his composition! Yes, there on the program were the words: FIRST SYMPHONY, by Peter Ilyich Tchaikovsky. The tears splashed over, and Peter could not read his own name.

Suddenly there was not a sound in the great hall as the conductor raised his arm. Then waves of his own music flowed over him, and Peter's heart beat so hard against his chest that he could scarcely breathe.

On and on the lilting melodies sang their songs, and when the last notes sounded their message, there was a storm of applause and cries of "Tchaikovsky! Tchaikovsky!"

His friends gathered quickly around him.

"Peter! They are calling you! You must go to the stage at once!" they urged him.

"No, no, I cannot! These old clothes! I would surely die!"

Firmly they took him by the arms and, pulling him to the stage door, pushed him to the platform.

Poor Peter. His knees shaking so that he could scarcely walk, and with battered hat in his hand, he ambled to the row of bright lights.

"Tchaikovsky! Bravo, Tchaikovsky!" The cheers and clapping rang jubilantly in his ears.

Awkwardly Peter bowed and, turning blindly, stumbled from the stage. Out into the cold he fled, where he could be alone with the night. On and on he walked, the drifted snow crunching hard under his old, worn boots. The tears froze on his cheeks as he lifted his face to the jeweled stars over his head.

"Thank you, God. You have been so kind to me. But I will write even better music," he promised. "I will write the songs of my people,–work songs, dance songs, songs of sorrow, and bright songs of happiness, until all the people of Russia have spoken."

CHAPTER TWO

In the sputtering candlelight, Peter lifted the lid of the old coin box and slipped in the last few kopeks.

"Enough and to spare, old tyrant!" he chuckled. Crawling under the thin blanket, he smiled at the thought of the secret that he had been keeping these long months. The pleasures that lay ahead danced through his dreams, until the pale June light sent him bounding from his cot.

"This is the day, the day, the day," he chanted, and shouldering his small bundle, he was off to join his younger brother.

"Petia!" At the first stop, the dear familiar call rang through the carriage as a tall handsome student eagerly searched the faces of the passengers. The next moment Peter's arm was about the slender shoulders.

"Think of it, Modia–we go to beautiful Finland to spend long weeks together! And see the fortune for our fine excursion!"

Banknotes and coins flew onto the seat between them. Months of hard, patient saving it meant, going without meals and giving extra lessons late at night.

In high spirits they rode along, and halfway to the border of Finland, just as they were about to change coaches, Peter's keen ears heard sounds of music.

"Oh, what a melody! Quickly, we must find the singer," he cried.

At the edge of the crowd, a tall keeper in yellow pantaloons sang a quaint old song as he led a roly-poly cub bear through his tricks. Only when there were tidbits would he perform, and now that his master's pockets were empty, down he sat, a stubborn, round ball of fur.

"Hurry, Modia! Take the coins and buy food for the little animal so that I can capture the song."

The last notes safely down, a startled cry brought Peter to attention.

"Look! The coach has gone on without us! "

In dismay they peered down the lonely roadway.

"Ah, well, no need to worry. Now there is plenty of time to explore the town."

"But the tickets, Petia?"

"A simple matter to purchase new ones, dear brother."

Off went the travelers, amusing themselves at every turn. Suddenly the odor of roasting meats took them into an inn.

"Do have the tasty stew, Modia, and then the roast beef and a bit of chicken. A delicious sweet will end the feast."

A feast it was, indeed, and sighing with pleasure, the two sauntered along the street, stopping to gaze into shop windows.

"That handsome coat would suit you well, Modia. And what an excellent timepiece! You shall have them both." Peter pressed everything in sight on his younger brother, until he became very uneasy.

"But the funds, Petia. They will not go on forever."

"Funds? Enough for the whole summer, with a little care."

When at last they arrived in Finland, Peter turned out his pockets and gasped in dismay. "Why–where–how ... I must have lost a great many banknotes!" he cried. His heart sank within him. "Ah, Modia, we shall have to turn back at once. Our adventure seems to be nearing an end."

A sudden idea made him brighten. "We could pay a little visit to our family in St. Petersburg!"

But when they stood before the old house door, it was to find it heavily barred for the summer.

"Six, seven, eight." Peter counted the last store of coins. "Just enough to take us to Alexandra, who will rescue her poor wandering brothers."

It was early evening when they arrived at the fine old estate, a bright voice calling above the barking watchdogs.

"Petia! What a delightful surprise! And Modia with you? Come, dear children, you must be starving."

The days stretched into beautiful long weeks, with merry picnics and boating and evenings of music.

"See, my queen, the piano pieces are finished," declared Peter, seating himself at the fine instrument to play his "Song Without Words."

Allegretto

With delighted cries at the beautiful music, Alexandra flung her arms about her beloved brother.

"Petia, I shall lock you here in my castle where you can be comfortable and compose the rest of your days."

"Ah, my guardian angel, you would not keep me for long. Rubinstein would come thundering to my hideaway and drag me back by the very hair of my head. In truth, I could never desert him now."

Suddenly a smile lighted his handsome face.

"You cannot imagine who is coming to Moscow to conduct his own music! The great composer Berlioz!"

It was indeed something to look forward to, and Peter counted the days until the concert night. In his carefully brushed old clothing, he sat in the great hall, listening closely to every note of the music of the master. The applause was ringing around him as hastily he strode backstage to be closer to the man who had written the beautiful compositions.

"Sir, I am Peter Tchaikovsky, and I wanted to thank you for the glory of this night."

"Peter Tchaikovsky, the composer?" Berlioz shook hands warmly. "It is I who want to thank you for your music! The way you write for instruments of the orchestra is so new and daring. Such color and excitement there is in it. Yes, yes, I play it often."

Peter's heart soared within him as he walked home.

"Nicholas, it is so good to hear the compositions of others," he declared to his friend. "If only I could travel to foreign lands and stay long enough to know their music, how much I would learn."

The director nodded briskly. "Why not give a concert of your works and raise funds for your heart's desire? Your many friends would be glad to give their services,—a singer, the orchestra, and a quartet."

Peter's eyes began to glow.

"Ah, yes, the quartet!" His hand went to his head. "But the music is not even begun!"

There was not a moment to lose. But how would he begin the composition? Yes! There was the haunting melody that he had heard at his sister's estate. Peter smiled as he thought of the sunny day when the strains of an old folk song wove a magic spell over the garden. So beautiful was the tune that Peter held his breath, fearful of missing a single sound. Leaning from the window, he spied a workman with trowel in hand, busily plastering a shed nearby.

"Oh, my good man, tell me where you found the splendid song!"

The workman shrugged, "Who knows?" and drew from his pocket his lunch of coarse black bread.

"If you will sing it again, I will bring you fish, and plenty of good wine to wash it down."

"Gladly, master! As many times as you wish."

In his little black notebook, Peter came quickly upon the plaintive strains. How right they would be for the second part of the quartet, the quiet, gentle Andante.

At last all was in readiness, the new quartet finished and rehearsed by the four fine musicians, the soprano who would sing Peter's lovely song, "None but the Lonely Heart", and the members of the orchestra to play the symphony.

But alas, although the evening's music was warmly applauded, the hall that Peter had chosen was so small that the funds would never take him on the longed-for journey.

"Patience, Tchaikovsky," Rubinstein comforted. "The time will come for traveling."

This happy little waltz of Peter's you may be able to play.

WALTZ

"Saint–Saëns is coming!" Peter was delighted at the news, and when the celebrated composer arrived in Moscow, the two became fast friends.

One evening, seated at a small café, the stocky little Frenchman laughed at Peter's tale of dancing all night long for a simple meal at an inn.

"Ah, then you, too, must love the ballet," exclaimed the bearded Camille. "I so much like the dance, that my father he always say to me, 'One more fancy step and I take the feet from the shoe!'"

Rubinstein, joining the two, listened in amusement. "Come, come, my light–footed gentlemen, you waste your time here. Let us be off to the conservatory, where you can test your rare talents."

To Nicholas's music around and around the brightly-lighted stage danced the two men, whirling on toes, leaping in air, and ending with low bows. Rubinstein laughed until the tears ran down his cheeks.

"If only the people of Moscow could witness such a spectacle, you would both be more famous than you already are!" he cried.

Through the years Peter went on working, longing for a little place where he could live in peace. It was coming now, sooner than he ever would have dreamed.

One afternoon, as the director sat in his little study, two young teachers suddenly appeared before him.

"We come to the defense of our friend, Tchaikovsky," they announced firmly. "Something will happen if he does not have a place to call home."

Rubinstein paced the floor, scowling at the two.

"But he is quite content here," he argued. "And far too lonely he would be, off by himself."

"Peter must decide that, sir," came the ready answer. "We discovered a little place for him only this morning. We move him tonight."

Before the startled Nicholas could reply, they were on their way. There was much to be done in finding a servant for a few kopeks and putting the new home in readiness before darkness set in. But at last their tasks were ended, and hurrying back to the conservatory, they knocked on Peter's door.

"Friend or foe?" a gruff voice called out.

"Wild ogres, demanding that you take a short walk, sir."

"Ah, my dear friends!" Peter flung wide the door, his face beaming. "Nothing like a brisk tramp to raise a man's spirits, yes?"

The three strode happily along and soon found themselves before a quaint old house, its blue shutters sagging in the dim light.

"A little surprise for you, Professor Tchaikovsky. We place in your hands the key to your new home."

With a startled cry, Peter turned on the two, his face paling.

"Surely–surely you would never play such a joke on me?"

"Enter, friend, and see for yourself!"

With a turn of the key they pushed him inside, where flickering candles lighted three tiny rooms. From the shadows, an old bent servant in faded coat bowed in greeting.

"Welcome, master. I care for you now. You like me, sir?"

Peter could not see for blinding tears as his hands gently touched the walls.

"My dream house! You have found this wonderful place for me to live in peace!" His arms were around the faithful friends, and the three burst into sudden cheering, to the astonishment of the old servant.

In a daze Peter explored his small castle, arranging again and again the tiny sofa and three stiff chairs. Never would he be happier, his whole life long. Now the days were like a dream, with someone to make his cot and cook a simple supper of soup in his own little home.

In thankfulness one day, this little composition came from his pen.

MORNING PRAYER

And now Peter's luck was changing and funds were growing ever larger, with payments from the rich Madame von Meck for music that he arranged for her to play. But try as he would to save, the funds had a way of disappearing.

On his daily walks, poor little peasant children came to know his favorite pathways, and when he returned home, not a single coin was left in his pockets.

One sunny afternoon, his two good friends arrived at his creaking door for a little visit.

"So, my gay companions of the road, let us be off and enjoy God's sweet nature world," he suggested eagerly.

Slipping off to the coin box in the kitchen, he found it almost empty.

"Kashkin! Tanyieff!" he called. "Let me have any funds that you may have with you. I will return all to you soon. "

Off went the three, and coming to a little bridge, Peter announced quietly, "I will explore a bit and rejoin you just beyond the river."

He chuckled to himself as he climbed down the bank. "At least I have outwitted the little beggars atop the span!" Hiding in the bushes for a moment, he was soon lost in the thick underbrush.

Suddenly from the tall grasses a swarm of urchins pounced on him from all sides, shouting at the top of their lungs.

"Caught in the trap! Your money or prison dungeon!" Grubby hands were thrust at him, and with sheepish grin, Peter emptied his pockets. Up and over the bridge the little beggars pushed their captive, to be met by the howling band of posted spies.

Kashkin and Tanyieff watched, horrified.

"So you would fool us, too! And all of our funds gone, as well as your own!"

Peter laughed feebly. "Ah well, it is good to feed hungry little ones. Besides, my own desires are so few."

Always Peter was to give away half of the funds that came

to him, complaining that he was too rich when the purse was full.

It was not too long, now, before the greatest wish of his heart was to be fulfilled, the longing to travel to faraway countries and drink in their music.

Peter could not believe the great good fortune that came to him one morning, with the promise from Madame von Meck of a large sum each year to care for all of his needs.

"My prayers have been answered!" His lips formed the words that came from deep within him. "And all through a real fairy godmother!"

In a frenzy of joy he found a quiet house in the country, with a beautiful forest of trees where he could roam through sunlight and shadow. And with a faithful servant, Alexis, who was to care for him all the rest of his days, his happiness knew no bounds.

His heart overflowing with happiness, he seized his pen one morning and scribbled a hasty note.

Dear Modia,
    Join me at once. I am rich beyond measure. We are off to see the world. Hasten!

PETIA

CHAPTER THREE

"Winter in Venice, and the water not turned to ice!" Peter looked in wonder at the canals leading in every direction. "And to think, Modia, of riding through the streets in a boat!"

Laughing in bewilderment, they turned to watch Modeste's small deaf and dumb pupil, Kolia, who stood proudly beside the gondolier, pushing with all his might against the heavy oar. The singing boatman patted the golden head and swung the gondola under the bridge.

"The small one tears at my heart," sighed Peter. "To think that never will he hear the sound of music his whole life long!"

"But he is happy in his own way. And an excellent little traveler, and easy to teach, Petia. A good thing his parents are pleased."

Suddenly the boat swerved to the right, just missing another craft, and sending the passengers reeling.

"Careful, Kolia! Kolia!" Peter waved his arms and ran along the slippery deck. But the warning came too late. In a flash, the little figure had slid over the side of the boat into the water.

"Save him! Save the little one!" The frenzied cries echoed through the canal as gondoliers dove after the small boy.

The few minutes seemed like hours before heads bobbed again on the sparkling surface.

"There he is! Thank God he is saved!"

Peter tore off his coat to wrap around the shivering lad as they raced back to their quarters for dry clothing.

"He seems none the worse for his adventure," he declared, pulling the blanket more closely about the child on his knees. "A good sleep, and he may be ready for pigeon feeding in the great square."

And fun it was to roam in the sunny open place before the cathedral. Hurdy-gurdies with lively monkeys were everywhere, and Peter followed their owners to capture a melody now and then.

"Have you noticed, Modeste, how everyone sings in this land of Italy? And the people so happy, even though many are poor."

To think that his dream had come true at last, and he could listen to the music of other countries. Peter could hardly believe his good fortune as he sat in the concert hall with his brother, after Kolia was safely in bed for the night.

One morning the happy travelers made their way to the museum, and often the blue-eyed visitors stopped to explain the paintings to small Kolia. An odd sight it was to the people of Venice, and they gathered in groups to watch the strangers waving long arms and speaking in a foreign tongue.

Looking up suddenly, Peter quickly led the way to the door.

"It is the same here as in Genoa. Perhaps we had better take the small one to our lodgings for a bit of food."

But no sooner had they reached the hotel than a sea of faces greeted them.

"There he is! It is the composer, himself! Yes, yes, it is the Russian musician, Tchaikovsky!"

Fear clutched at Peter's heart. In a flash he escaped through the back door, Modeste and Kolia close behind. Down a side street they ran and, out of breath, stopped at a wayside inn.

"We cannot return until they have left," gasped Peter.

For two whole days they stayed away and late at night crept back to their rooms.

"This will never do. We cannot hide like this," Peter decided the next morning. "Besides, it is time we were in San Remo, where faithful Alexy is waiting to care for us."

It was good to arrive in the peaceful seaside town. With a sigh of contentment, Peter beamed on the little group as they sat on the small balcony, watching the sun slip gently behind the dark cypresses.

"I could stay here forever," he declared over Kolia's fair head, resting against him. "Everything is right for my work."

One afternoon, strolling alone in the hills, Peter turned

often to look back through the silvery olive trees to the deep blue waters beyond. At the glory spread around him, the melodious fourth symphony began to compose itself in his mind, and smiling, he sat to listen. It was good! He would set it down when he arrived at the lodge.

Striding along the hillside, he paused at a sight so beautiful, he could not believe it to be true. The little glade at his feet was filled to overflowing with velvety giant violets.

"A sea of blue!" he cried aloud. "Like a piece of the sky suddenly fallen in this one little place!"

He was on his knees, breathlessly picking the long-stemmed blooms. Filling his pockets and hat and with hands overflowing, he ran all the way back to town.

"Kolia! Come, dear child, you must help me arrange all of this beauty."

Happily he watched the lad as he touched the flowers so gently, his fair cheeks flushed with delight, strange sounds coming from his lips.

How he loved the boy, always bringing him little gifts, and taking him on short excursions, and crooning over him when a distressed look crossed the delicate face.

60

Everyone was happy, excepting poor Alexis, who hovered over his charges, doing little services, but longing to be back in his homeland.

One morning he awakened the whole household with loud cries, and hurrying to his small room, Peter looked in dismay at the large spots covering his body.

"O Master! Master!" gasped Alexis. "It is from too little to do. There is no wood to chop in San Remo!"

Peter called the doctor at once and through the day and night watched over the frightened servant, doing all that he could to make him comfortable.

"Another trouble we have, Modeste." Peter spoke in low tones. "Funds for food are at an end, and still no word from Madame von Meek."

Eagerly they watched the post and in sign language amused Kolia with stories through the anxious hours. The next morning, with a cry of joy, Peter tore open the letter brought by the innkeeper.

"Fifteen hundred francs! Dear, kind fairy god-mother has come to the rescue!" he cried. "As soon as Alexy is well enough, we go to Florence to celebrate."

"I pack at once!" came the reply from the bed, amid shouts of laughter.

Early morning found them on their way to the beautiful city.

"Is it not a magical place?" exulted Peter. "Let us see as much as we can while the day is still young. You are not too weary, little one?" he spoke with his hands to Kolia.

There was no time for an answer, with the first stirring notes of a song soaring across the square. So beautiful was the voice that the little group stood as if turned to stone.

When the last liquid note died away, Peter flew to the steps where a young boy sat with guitar on his knees, while his father hastily pocketed the shower of coins.

"Never have I heard a voice so pure," breathed Peter, his eyes bright with tears. "Like crystal water flowing."

That night, high above the city, as the waters of the Arno tumbled in the distance, Peter could not rest with the melody of the little singer echoing in his mind. There was only one way to still the sounds, and using the lilting strains of the folk tune, he composed the loveliest song and called it "Pimpinella."

Never content until he had filled some of the hours of the day with work, he found great delight in completing his fourth symphony.

"It is finished!" he cried, waving the papers in air. "A rousing cheer for my dearest child, ready to find its way in the world."

Hasn't this composition of Peter's a lovely, singing melody?

DREAMS

Andante

It was time, now, for Kolia to return to his parents, and with a warm hug for the boy whom he had come to love so well, Peter was on his way to pay a little visit to his beloved Alexandra.

The moon was riding high when he arrived at the vast farmland, and weary with long traveling, he stole quietly to bed and was soon in the land of dreams. But alas, not for too long.

"Uncle Petia! Petia! Petia!" Small voices were calling in the hallway as little fists beat steadily on his door.

"Hush, children! You must not waken him so early in the morning!" Alexandra and the nursemaids rushed after the young members of the household.

But it was too late. From his room stumbled the sleepy traveler, and with joyous shouts the children pounced upon him, pulling him to the floor and crawling over him with shrieks of laughter. Their mother sighed and shook her head at the tumbling heap.

"What do you do to make them love you so, Petia? But now you will be at their mercy for two whole days while I go off to the next town."

Peter grinned at her from the floor.

"They are in safe hands, dear sister. Go, with your pretty head at peace."

As the door closed behind her, he was on his knees in the center of the group.

"Shall we make a little ballet of the Sleeping Beauty, all set to music?"

"Yes! Yes! YES!"

Tatiana was the beautiful princess busy at her spinning wheel, to Peter's bright new music. The melodies told the story so exactly, it was easy enough to follow, from the pricking of the finger to the long, long sleep and the awakening kiss of the handsome prince.

"Tomorrow we will make Swan Lake into a ballet," promised Peter, as nursemaids came to tuck one and all into bed for a good rest.

No sooner was the big house quiet and Peter back in his room, setting down the first notes of the new Sleeping Beauty Ballet, than a loud scream sent him racing to the wide avenue behind the house.

"Oh, master, the mischievous little one stole away to ride his pony. I fear he is badly hurt!"

They came upon the frightened horseman in a shallow ditch at the side of the road, his round face covered with mud.

"There, there now, brave jockey," Peter comforted him, gently carrying the slender figure into the darkened room. "Uncle Petia will make you well."

Sitting beside the bed, he crooned old folk songs until the weeping was ended and the sorrowful rider safe in the land of dreams.

A few more notes of the ballet found their way onto the paper when shrieks of distress sent him flying to the kitchen, where a small girl, secretly in search of sweets, had caught her finger in the door.

"Oh, what a funny old fox!" Peter was on his knees, tying

up the hand in big wagging ears. "Now this perky gentleman was on his way to the fair, when suddenly he spied a mincing hen with basket on her arm. 'And where are you bound, this lovely day?' said he in sweetest tones. 'And what, pray tell, is in that hamper?' "

On went the story, the small listener with tearstained cheeks safe in Peter's arms, the hurt long forgotten.

But the troubles were not yet ended. In the middle of the night a frightened nursemaid was pounding on his door.

"It is the baby, sir. A bad case of croup, and the doctor miles away!"

Peter bent anxiously over the tiny form through the hours, bringing what comfort he could, with the aid of the patient servants. At last, with a prayer of thankfulness as the little one breathed easier, he stole off to bed for a bit of well-earned rest.

Home again late that night, Alexandra went in search of her brother. There, in the peaceful quiet, more of the ballet was finding its way on paper.

"The children, Petia?" she began anxiously.

His face wreathed in smiles, he looked up at her. "The little ones? All safe and well. Ah, my sweet sister, next to God come the children. And two new ballets they have inspired." He hummed bits of the lovely music and sighed.

"Heaven has been so kind! It is hard to believe that now I am free to compose and travel to my heart's content." He was silent a moment. "A beautiful life, but a restless one, as well. If I am not composing, the strongest desire comes over me to breathe the air of a new city."

Peter was to obey the thirst for travel all the rest of his days. Never a year went by without a visit to foreign lands.

One fine day, discovering himself in a fashionable Paris street, he stopped short and looked down at his shabby clothing.

"Why do I go about like a beggar when everyone I meet is dressed as a gentleman?" he scolded himself.

Into the nearest shop he took himself promptly.

"The best raiment possible," he ordered the startled clerk.

What a time he had, choosing from the coats, hats, shoes and linen scattered in piles around him. At last, dressed in all his finery, silken scarf and coral pin at his neck and lilac gloves on his hands, off he strolled into the bright sunshine, cane held jauntily in hand.

Enjoying a little supper at an outdoor café, on down the avenue he took himself. But what was this? Surely he must be dreaming! There, over the concert hall, in bold, shining lights was his name:

PETER TCHAIKOVSKY

Breathlessly he read the notice of the concert of his compositions to be played on Sunday afternoon. If only everyone at home could see the sign, how proud they would be!

Around the world his fame was spreading, slowly and surely, and everywhere musicians were conducting his music. Then why should he not lead orchestras in his own works? Back again in Russia, he spoke eagerly to the twins, who came to welcome him home.

"See, my dear children, another offer to conduct in St. Petersburg!" he cried. "If all goes well, I will be ready to lead orchestras elsewhere."

The night of the concert arrived, and as he walked quickly to the stage, thundering applause greeted him. Bowing low, he turned to the orchestra to lead the men in his symphony, a concerto, and a suite.

Wild Russian strains came thundering down on the listeners, changing suddenly to delicate harmonies, wistful and haunting, that spun themselves to faintest echo.

The audience shouted its joy, calling for its famous composer until the rafters rang with joyful cries.

"Tchaikovsky! Tchaikovsky! Tchaikovsky!"

News of his success spread rapidly, and offers to conduct came from far and near. Away in the country with Alexis,

Peter shook his head in amazement.

"Why, I must have led the orchestra better than I thought," he mused. "Think of it, Alexy–an international concert tour, with your master conducting!"

In a whirl of excitement he made himself ready and was soon off to Berlin where he delighted the German people with his music.

Happy beyond words at his success, Peter eagerly picked up the newspaper the next morning. But what was this! A luncheon in his honor that very day, with every notable present!

"Oh no, no!" Peter cried out in alarm. "I could never face such a gathering!"

With all speed he was on his way and soon found himself in Leipzig. How good it was to escape! And how truly he enjoyed the new city and the hours spent with the celebrated composers, Brahms and Grieg.

Concerts there were in Hamburg, Paris, London, and more happy meetings with famous music makers, Dvořák and Gounod and Massenet.

At last, after long months of traveling, back to his homeland Peter took himself, to bask in the peace and quiet

of his little home on the edge of the deep woods.

"Spring! It is spring, Alexy! Quickly–my old coat. I go walking among my beautiful trees. You may come too, old Sultan," he cried, patting the shaggy head of the stalwart watchdog. "But mind–no birds!"

"Company for dinner tonight, master?" Alexis stood in the doorway in his old faded apron.

"No, no. Not tonight. I work on the new symphony this afternoon. No visitors on working days."

Out in the bracing air, Peter sang a song of thanksgiving as he looked far over the fields that he loved so well. Tiny straw-roofed huts and a little church dotted the countryside, and breaking the stillness, the faint song of a lark made his heart leap for joy.

In this music that Peter wrote, you can hear the trilling of the little bird.

76

SONG OF THE LARK

80

Off into the woods he roamed, where the fifth symphony worked itself out in his mind. Scarcely knowing where he walked, Peter strode along, a faraway look in his keen blue eyes.

Two hours later, just as he was homeward bound, a sharp barking took him to a patch of thick underbrush. There, with one paw lifted, Sultan stood over a wounded baby rabbit, half buried in musty leaves.

"There now, little creature of God, do not be frightened," soothed Peter. "We will take you home and care for the dear broken leg." Carefully he slipped the soft little bundle into his pocket and patted the brown head at his side. "Good old Sultan! A special bone for your supper tonight."

The happy dog bounded ahead and waited patiently for his master at the gate.

"What a croaking voice you have," muttered Peter, pushing against the whining rusty hinges. "A bit of oil for you and a brushful of paint for the dingy sign." He read the words thoughtfully.

PETER I. TCHAIKOVSKY
RECEIVES MONDAYS AND THURSDAYS, 3 TO 5.
NOT AT HOME. PLEASE DO NOT RING.

Opening the sagging house door, he took the trembling baby rabbit from its warm nest. "Hurry, Alexy! We must bind up the poor little leg."

In a moment the two men were on their knees, fitting a tiny splint on the small ball of fur.

"Sultan will watch over you from now on," promised the master, tenderly carrying the bright-eyed creature to a bed in the corner.

The dog seemed to understand, and springing to his chair covered with old coats, he wound himself around his new companion, licking the tiny head now and then.

Peter stood smiling at the sight, when the sudden sound of footsteps took him to the door.

"Modeste! What a delightful surprise! Come in, come in,

dear brother!" His hands were outstretched in welcome.

"I bring happy news, Petia. The opera company is rehearsing your Sleeping Beauty Ballet. And so pleased are they, that they would like you to begin another at once. Here is the story."

Peter tore open the fat envelope and began to read. "Ah, a fairy tale. Listen, Modia, to the adventures of Mister Nutcracker.

"It is Christmas Eve in Nuremburg, and around the laden tree, Marie and her brother Fritz help to entertain the guests. An odd little man arrives with a strange gift, a German nutcracker in the shape of an old man, that he has carved for his favorite Marie.

"With delighted cries she crams nuts into the hungry mouth to watch the teeth crack them in a wonderful way. But Fritz is far too rough, and soon the poor nutcracker is broken. Marie is sad, indeed, and binding up the head of her little man, she puts him in the doll bed.

"That night she cannot sleep, and creeping down the stairs for another look at her favorite gift, she is frightened by the sound of mice swarming over the room. Before her startled eyes, the toys come to life and a dreadful battle begins. Her

dear nutcracker is about to be overcome by the giant mouse king when Marie throws her shoe at the horrible creature, finishing him on the spot.

"In the twinkling of an eye the nutcracker turns into a handsome prince and leads the way to a magic kingdom. Away they fly over the wintry forest through a cloud of lacy snowflakes, wondrous to behold."

Peter chuckled. "How delightful the tale. Now you will hear the second part, in the Kingdom of Sweets.

"Marie and her prince open the gate of almonds, on the pavement of macaroons, and wander into the forest of Christmas trees, where gold and silver fruits hang from snowy branches. On they roam past the river of orange juice to the village of sweet cake and the city of candied fruits, where clear palaces of sugar gleam in the sun.

"The Sugar Plum Fairy awaits Marie and her prince, who come sailing over the lake in a walnut shell boat. Seated on special thrones, they are entertained by dancers Hot Chocolate, Arabian coffee, and Chinese tea. Like a whirlwind,

on their toes come marzipan, striped candy canes, and a giant tea cozy lady, who keeps small sweets hidden under her wide skirts.

"With a gracious bow to the guests, the Sugar Plum Fairy begins her dance, and the festival ends when the fairest flowers of the garden join her in the loveliest waltz anyone could imagine.

"Marie and her prince bid farewell to the gathering and sail away in their walnut shell, alone on the rippling blue waters."

Peter laid aside the fairy tale, his face alight.

"Ah, Modeste, what delicate, airy music I must write, to fit the characters exactly. I can hear it now. The children will enjoy the ballet, as well as grown-ups."

In a few months he was hard at work on the music, when in bounded his friend Kashkin one morning, covered with snow from head to foot.

"Well, well! The cozy workman I find, holed up in his den!" he growled playfully, peeling off his greatcoat. "If you or your man would clear a pathway to your door, the outside could come inside! I present you, Mister Mole, with your mail!"

Peter laughed heartily and opened the letter with a foreign stamp. But the next moment the papers fluttered to the floor.

"Kashkin! I could never accept! Think of conducting orchestras in America, where Indians and fierce animals prowl the streets! And the mighty ocean to cross—I would surely be drowned!"

But with all his fears, Peter made ready and took himself to Paris to wait for the boat to set sail. One morning, as he explored an old part of the city, what should he discover but a new instrument called the celesta, played as a piano, but sounding like bells.

The very thing for the fairy music in the Nutcracker Ballet! He must secure it at all costs and keep it a deep secret for use in the orchestra.

But the joy of his discovery was soon ended as he boarded the steamship and put out to sea in a fierce gale. Poor Peter! He took to his bed in great fright and shivered and shook under the bedcovers.

"Why did I come on this journey? Oh, why did I leave my snug, safe home?" he wailed, as the ship shuddered and rolled through the days and nights.

Never was anyone so glad to feel the ground under his feet when at last he landed in New York harbor. And how friendly were the kind people who came to meet him, with nowhere an animal or wild Indian in sight.

"We are at your service, Master Tchaikovsky. What can we do to make you comfortable? You must give us the pleasure of dining with us," sounded on all sides.

Peter shook his head in amazement. If only he were not so homesick, how happy he would be in this wonderful land of warmhearted citizens.

The honor of opening the new Carnegie Hall was great, indeed, and with so fine an orchestra, he must conduct well, especially his own Marche Solennelle.

The night of the concert, the applause was deafening as he was called again and again to the people who were standing to do him honor. Why, he was even more famous in America than at home!

Walter Damrosch, a fine musician, grasped his hand in warm clasp when the fourth concert came to an end.

"Ah, Master Tchaikovsky, you have given us pleasure we shall never forget." he declared earnestly. As Peter left the hall, he went on: "Never have I met a great composer so gentle and modest. From the very first moment we all loved him."

It was true. Even on the streets, little children, grandmothers, men, and women, followed him wherever he went. Peter smiled into the glowing faces, his blue eyes twinkling.

"Just like Moscow," he said to himself. "Everyone follows me there, too. I wonder why. Ah, if only I were not so homesick! But now a concert in Baltimore and Philadelphia, and back to my native land I fly!"

What excitement there was on his return. The twins and Kashkin and Tanyieff were all awaiting him, their joyous cries ringing heartily.

"Welcome home! Welcome! Welcome!"

Peter beamed on the bright faces gathered around the table, ready to share the blazing celebration pudding.

"Ah, my angels, one thing I have learned well. In every country around the wide world, people are good, with kind and gentle hearts."

Late into the night he talked on and on, telling of his adventures in the strange and wonderful land of America.

The next morning, as he waited for hot tea, low whining and scratching took Peter to the door.

"Bless my soul!" There, wagging his tail proudly stood Sultan, and beside him, two brown baby puppies falling over each other in their eagerness to reach the master.

"Oh, the little beauties!" With a cry of delight, Peter was on his knees, gathering up the tiny bundles. "But where is the mother? Sultan, go find the mother!"

But with all their searching, never did they discover the owner, and with great joy, Peter added the new members to his household.

Each morning Sultan proudly took his young charges for a walk in the garden, pushing them along with his nose or

sending them flying with his paw, to the amusement of Peter and Modeste in the doorway.

Suddenly Peter strode to the piano, and putting his hands on the keys, challenging music rang out. Wonderful it was, indeed, like the call of fate to the whole world. Wheeling around, he called, "Modia! Hear the opening of my new symphony. What shall we call it–the sixth?"

"But it is a bit sad, Petia. Why not name it Tragic Symphony?"

"No, no–not Tragic."

Thoughtfully Modeste sipped a glass of fragrant tea. "Then how about Pathétique?"

"Yes! Bravo, Modia! You have named it well. We will call it the Pathétique Symphony."

Through the years of work and travel, honors fell in showers on the master. But the more honors, the more he longed to hide away in his beloved house and garden.

Now the English people were calling him to their country to confer on him their highest award, the Doctor of Music. Surely he could not refuse.

With a sigh, into the bag went his special conducting clothes, carefully packed by Alexis, while Sultan nosed uneasily about. He seemed to know that his master would be gone on a longer journey than usual, and whining and lifting his paw for the usual hand-shake, he would not leave Peter's side.

"Good, faithful Sultan. A little business with the Kingdom of Great Britain, and I'll soon be back. And see that you keep close watch on the dear Klin house while I'm away."

With a warm pat on the brown head, the master was off.

Never could he have dreamed of a finer celebration awaiting him. In the English capital he discovered his old friend, Saint–Saëns, and the two clasped hands warmly.

"What joy to find you here, Camille! A long stretch from the stage where we danced a royal ballet together, yes?"

But serious, indeed, was Peter as he conducted his own works for the London gathering. Then out to the University of Cambridge he took himself, to be gowned in splendid robe of scarlet and white silk, a velvet cap with gold tassels on his head.

Down the street he walked with the noted composers Saint–Saëns, Boito, and Bruch, cheering throngs lining the streets.

At the head of the procession strode a portly maharaja in jeweled headdress and diamond necklace gleaming in the sun. On through the city he led the celebrated band to the platform, where Peter was proudly proclaimed a Doctor of Music.

96

In his few words of English, he tried to give his thanks.

"My melodies must say to you what is in the heart," he murmured and, with brisk nods, was on his way back to London.

Home, home, home! The word was dearer to him than ever before and sang in his mind as the miles took him ever closer to his native land.

As he neared little Klin, he gazed long from the train window. The endless Russian steppes were greener than when he had left; the sun shone much brighter. The seeds that he had planted in his little garden would be sending up tender shoots by now.

Would old Sultan remember him? Ah, there was the dear Klin house and a bounding, trembling, furry mass hurling itself against him.

"Sultan! Good old Sultan! To think that you might have forgotten me!"

Peter Ilyich Tchaikovsky, the greatest master of Russian music, was at home again.

The Story of Peter Tchaikovsky is part of *Music Appreciation: Book 2 for the Middle Grades.*

Music Appreciation: Book 2 for the Middle Grades (for grades 5 to 8) will introduce older children to seven different composers, dating from 1810 to 1908 (Chopin, Schumann, Wagner, Foster, Brahms, Tchaikovsky and MacDowell). Each composer's childhood and adult life are vividly described in individual biographies. Every important incident is mentioned and every detail of the stories is true. Each book contains written music and delightful pictures throughout. It is more than the human side of these books that will make them live, for in the music the great masters breathe.

The Student Book incorporates activities from across the curriculum and promotes an increased knowledge of and appreciation for classical music and the composers. Geared for a variety of learners—auditory, kinesthetic, visual, and just plain "active"—it is user-friendly for multi-age groups.

<u>Titles used in this curriculum are:</u>
Frederic Chopin, Early Years
Frederic Chopin, Later Years
Robert Schumann and Mascot Ziff
Adventures of Richard Wagner
Stephen Foster and His Little Dog Tray
The Young Brahms
The Story of Peter Tchaikovsky
Peter Tchaikovsky and the Nutcracker Ballet
Edward MacDowell and His Cabin in the Pines

For more information visit our website at www.Zeezok.com

Also available from Zeezok Publishing:

Music Appreciation: Book 1 for the Elementary Grades (for grades 1 to 6) will introduce children to seven different composers, dating from 1685 to 1828 (Bach, Handel, Haydn, Mozart, Beethoven, Paganini and Schubert). Each composer's childhood and adult life are vividly described in individual biographies. Every important incident is mentioned and every detail of the stories is true. Each book contains written music and delightful pictures throughout. It is more than the human side of these books that will make them live, for in the music the great masters breathe.

The Student Activity book includes a variety of hands-on activities such as: geography lessons, history lessons, recipes, instrument studies, music vocabulary, hand writing, musical facts of the Classical period, timelines, character trait studies, and so much more. Geared for a variety of learners—auditory, kinesthetic, visual, and just plain "active"—the Student Activity Book is an excellent companion to your reading experience.

<u>Titles used in this curriculum are:</u>
Sebastian Bach, The Boy from Thuringia
Handel at the Court of Kings
Joseph Haydn, The Merry Little Peasant
Mozart, The Wonder Boy
Ludwig Beethoven and the Chiming Tower Bells
Paganini, Master of Strings
Franz Schubert and His Merry Friends

For more information visit our website at www.Zeezok.com

CPSIA information can be obtained
at www.ICGtesting.com
Printed in the USA
BVOW07s0937011217

501545BV00054B/1803/P